Easy Croquette Cookbook

50 Delicious Croquette Recipes

By
BookSumo Press
All rights reserved

Published by
http://www.booksumo.com

ENJOY THE RECIPES?
KEEP ON COOKING WITH 6 MORE FREE COOKBOOKS!

Visit our website and simply enter your email address to join the club and receive your 6 cookbooks.

http://booksumo.com/magnet

https://www.instagram.com/booksumopress/

https://www.facebook.com/booksumo/

LEGAL NOTES

All Rights Reserved. No Part Of This Book May Be Reproduced Or Transmitted In Any Form Or By Any Means. Photocopying, Posting Online, And / Or Digital Copying Is Strictly Prohibited Unless Written Permission Is Granted By The Book's Publishing Company. Limited Use Of The Book's Text Is Permitted For Use In Reviews Written For The Public.

Table of Contents

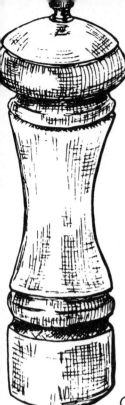

Star of the Sea Tuna Croquettes 7

Grandma's Simply Salmon Croquettes 8

Moroccan Croquettes of Spicy Red Lentils 9

Brazilian Cheese Croquettes 10

November's Turkey Croquettes 11

Ohio Noodle Croquettes 12

Ground Beef Croquettes 14

Country Dinner Mashed Potato and Onion Croquettes 15

Cajun Cornmeal Tilapia Croquettes 16

Latin American Croquettes 17

Vegetarian Spicy Parsnip Croquettes 18

Croquettes Japanese Style 19

Shrimp and Rice Croquettes 20

Tuscan Croquettes 21

Mashed Potatoes Green Onions and Bacon Croquettes 22

Mediterranean Mashed Potato Croquettes 23

Country Honey Turkey and Swiss Croquettes 24

Simply Italian Cheese Croquettes 25

Fiesta Croquettes 26

Cheddar Halibut Croquettes 28

Croquettes Asian Style 29

Turkey, Mushrooms, and Spice Croquettes 30

Roasted Red Pepper and Chickpea Croquettes 32

Fall-Time Pumpkin Croquettes 33

Irish Dinner Croquettes 34

Cheddar and Aubergine Croquettes 35

Mexican Croquettes 36

European Veal Croquettes 37

Pinto Beans and Carrot Croquettes 39

Zucchini Croquettes Southern Greek Style 40

New England Curry Crab Croquettes 41

Rustic Spanish Croquettes 42

French Spinach Croquettes 44

Mustard Curry Ground Beef Croquettes with Sauce 45

Southern Black-Eyed Pea Croquettes 47

October's Turkey and Celery Croquettes 48

Minced Mushroom and Rice Croquettes 49

Corned Beef and Sauerkraut Croquettes 50

Nutmeg Croquettes 51

Cranberry Croquettes 52

Spicy Leftover Rice Croquettes 53

Wild Game Croquettes 54

English Cheese Croquettes 56

Tomato and Ricotta Italian Croquettes 57

Sunday Morning Sausage Croquette 58

Florida Clam Croquettes 60

Arabian Chickpeas and Chives Croquettes 61

Vegetarian Dream Croquettes 62

New England Cod Croquettes 63

Star of the Sea
Tuna Croquettes

Prep Time: 10 mins
Total Time: 25 mins

Servings per Recipe: 4
Calories	249.3
Fat	7.7g
Cholesterol	128.7mg
Sodium	379.0mg
Carbohydrates	15.3g
Protein	29.9g

Ingredients

- 2 (6 oz.) cans canned tuna
- 1 C. wheat germ (untoasted)
- 2 eggs, lightly beaten
- 2 - 3 tbsp tomato juice
- 1 - 2 tbsp fresh dill, chopped
- black pepper, to taste
- cooking oil

Directions

1. In a large bowl, add all the ingredients and mix well.
2. Make 4 equal sized patties from the mixture.
3. In a heavy frying pan, heat 1-2 tbsp oil and fry the patties till golden brown from both sides.
4. Transfer the patties onto a paper towel lined plate to drain.

GRANDMA'S Simply Salmon Croquettes

Prep Time: 10 mins
Total Time: 30 mins

Servings per Recipe: 6
Calories   277.8
Fat   11.1g
Cholesterol   123.7mg
Sodium   477.2mg
Carbohydrates   22.5g
Protein   20.8g

Ingredients

1 (14 oz.) cans salmon, drained
1 medium onion (grated)
salt and pepper
1/4 C. flour
1 1/2 C. milk
1/4 tsp garlic powder
1 C. seasoned bread crumbs
2 eggs, beaten
2 tbsp butter
sunflower oil (for frying)

Directions

1. In a large frying pan, melt the butter on medium-high heat and sauté the onion and garlic powder till tender.
2. Add the salmon, salt and pepper and cook till heated completely.
3. Add the flour and stir till well combined.
4. Slowly, add the milk, stirring continuously till the mixture becomes thick and forms a ball.
5. Transfer the mixture into a plate and keep aside to cool completely.
6. Make oval shaped croquettes from the mixture.
7. Dip the croquettes in beaten eggs and then coat with the bread crumbs.
8. In a deep skillet, heat the oil and deep fry till golden brown from both sides.
9. Transfer the croquettes onto a paper towel lined plate to drain.

Moroccan Croquettes of Spicy Red Lentils

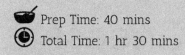 Prep Time: 40 mins
Total Time: 1 hr 30 mins

Servings per Recipe: 6
Calories	253.2
Fat	11.9g
Cholesterol	35.2mg
Sodium	24.7mg
Carbohydrates	26.6g
Protein	253.2g

Ingredients

1 C. split red lentils, washed
1 green bell pepper, washed, seeded and chopped finely
1 red onion, chopped finely
2 garlic cloves, finely minced
1 tsp garam masala
1/2 tsp chili powder
1 tsp cumin powder
2 tsp lemon juice
2 tbsp peanuts, toasted without salt and coarsely chopped
2 1/2 C. water
1 egg, beaten
3 tbsp all-purpose flour
1 tsp ground turmeric
1 tsp chili powder
4 tbsp peanut oil
salt and pepper, to taste

Directions

1. In a large pan, add the red lentils, bell pepper, onion, garlic, garam masala, chili powder, cumin powder, lemon juice, peanuts and water and bring to a boil.
2. Reduce the heat and simmer for about 30 minutes, stirring occasionally.
3. Remove from heat and keep aside to cool slightly.
4. Add the egg, salt and pepper and beat well.
5. Now, let the mixture cool completely.
6. In a small plate, mix together the flour, turmeric and chili powder.
7. Make the circles from the lentil mixture and coat with the flour mixture evenly.
8. In a skillet, heat the oil and cook the croquettes in batches till browned from both sides.
9. Serve immediately with chutney or a crisp salad.

BRAZILIAN Cheese Croquettes

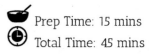

Prep Time: 15 mins
Total Time: 45 mins

Servings per Recipe: 4
Calories   249.4
Fat   15.0g
Cholesterol   88.8mg
Sodium   244.6mg
Carbohydrates   21.1g
Protein   7.1g

Ingredients

2 oz. butter, cubed
2/3 C. flour
1 egg, separated
1/4 C. breadcrumbs
1/4 C. Parmesan cheese, grated
salt and pepper, as needed
1 tbsp water
chili, salsa for serving

Directions

1. Set your oven to 350 degrees F before doing anything else and generously, grease a baking sheet.
2. In a bowl, add the flour and butter and with your hands rub till a coarse mixture forms.
3. Add the egg yolk, breadcrumbs, Parmesan cheese, salt, pepper and water and mix till well combined.
4. Make golf ball sized balls from the mixture.
5. Dip the balls into slightly beaten egg white and arrange onto the prepared baking sheet in a single layer.
6. Cook in the oven for about 25 minutes.
7. Serve warm alongside the chili salsa.

November's Turkey Croquettes

Prep Time: 10 mins
Total Time: 4 hrs 10 mins

Servings per Recipe: 4
Calories   513.7
Fat   30.1g
Cholesterol   155.4mg
Sodium   1219.8mg
Carbohydrates   29.4g
Protein   29.8g

Ingredients

- 2 - 3 C. cooked turkey, chopped up (leftovers)
- 2 C. prepared stuffing (leftovers)
- 2 eggs, slightly beaten
- flour, for dredging
- breadcrumbs, for dredging
- 3 tbsp vegetable oil, for frying
- SAUCE, OR USE GRAVY:
- 1 (12 oz.) can condensed cream of chicken soup
- 1/2 C. 2% low-fat milk

Directions

1. In a bowl, mix together the turkey, stuffing and eggs and refrigerate for about 3 hours minimum.
2. With about 3/4 C. of the mixture, make a log.
3. Place the log onto a smooth surface and flatten the bottom into 3x2-inch thickness.
4. Coat the croquettes with the flour and then with the bread crumbs.
5. Heat the oil in deep skillet on medium heat and fry the croquettes about 10-15 minutes, turning occasionally.
6. Meanwhile for the sauce in pan, mix together the can of soup and 1/2 C. of the milk and cook till warmed and creamy, stirring continuously.
7. Pour the sauce over the croquettes.

OHIO NOODLE
Croquettes

🥣 Prep Time: 40 mins
⏱ Total Time: 1 hr 10 mins

Servings per Recipe: 12
Calories   200.5
Fat   10.5g
Cholesterol   87.0mg
Sodium   204.9mg
Carbohydrates   18.8g
Protein   7.6g

Ingredients

1 (8 oz.) packages noodles
6 tbsp butter
3 tbsp chopped green onions
6 tbsp flour
1/4 tsp salt
1/8 tsp white pepper
2 C. milk
1/2 C. parmesan cheese

1 egg, beaten
flour
2 eggs, beaten with 2 tbsp water
panko breadcrumbs
vegetable oil (for frying)

Directions

1. Grease a 9-inch square baking dish.
2. In a large pan of the boiling water, prepare the noodles according to the package's directions.
3. Meanwhile in a medium pan, melt the butter and sauté the green onions till softened.
4. Stir in the flour, salt and white pepper and cook till bubbly.
5. Stir in the milk and cook till thick and bubbly, stirring continuously.
6. Add the Parmesan cheese and stir till melted.
7. Add a little of the cheese mixture into the beaten egg and stir to combine.
8. Return the egg mixture to pan and bring to a boil.
9. Drain the noodles well and transfer into a bowl.
10. Pour the sauce over the noodles and mix well.
11. Transfer the mixture into the prepared baking dish and press to smooth the top surface.
12. With a piece of foil, cover the top, pressing down over the noodles.
13. Refrigerate to chill for overnight. Before serving, place flour egg-water mixture and Panko crumbs in separate shallow dishes.

14. Set your oven to 375 degrees F.
15. Cut the chilled noodle mixture into squares.
16. Coat the squares with the flour, then with egg mixture, then with Panko crumbs, covering all sides thoroughly.
17. In a deep skillet, heat the oil to 375 and fry the squares in batches for about 2-3 minutes.
18. Transfer the croquettes onto a paper towel lined plate to drain
19. Serve hot.

GROUND BEEF
Croquettes

Prep Time: 20 mins
Total Time: 35 mins

Servings per Recipe: 2
Calories   398.7
Fat   14.5g
Cholesterol   30.5mg
Sodium   609.4mg
Carbohydrates   56.9g
Protein   10.6g

Ingredients

1 onion, chopped fine
2 tbsp melted butter
1 C. breadcrumbs
salt
pepper
nutmeg
Maggi seasoning, to taste
2 tbsp chopped fresh parsley

1/2 lb ground beef
1 egg white, lightly beaten with a small amount of water
1 - 2 C. breadcrumbs, for coating
vegetable oil (for frying, about 1/2 inch in the pan)

Directions

1. In a large pan, melt the butter and sauté the onion till tender.
2. Add 1 C. of the breadcrumbs, salt, pepper, nutmeg, Maggi seasonings, parsley, beef and beef and mix well.
3. Remove from the heat make 8 cylinder shaped croquettes.
4. Coat the croquettes with the breadcrumbs, then dip in the egg white and finally coat with the bread crumbs again.
5. In a deep skillet, heat the oil and cook the croquette till golden brown.
6. Serve hot alongside the French fries and salad.

Country Dinner
Mashed Potato and Onion Croquettes

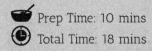

Prep Time: 10 mins
Total Time: 18 mins

Servings per Recipe: 4
Calories   263.9
Fat   10.7g
Cholesterol   51.9mg
Sodium   541.6mg
Carbohydrates   33.8g
Protein   7.8g

Ingredients

- 2 C. mashed potatoes
- 2 tbsp minced onions
- 1 egg, slightly beaten
- 3 tbsp grated parmesan cheese
- 2 tbsp parsley, minced
- 3/4 C. breadcrumbs
- 2 tbsp vegetable oil

Directions

1. In a bowl, add the potato, onion, egg, cheese and parsley and mix till well combined.
2. Make 8 equal sized patties from the mixture and refrigerate till serving.
3. Coat the croquettes with the breadcrumbs evenly.
4. In a deep skillet, heat the oil on medium heat and cook the croquette for about 4 minutes.
5. Serve hot.

CAJUN CORNMEAL
Tilapia Croquettes

Prep Time: 15 mins
Total Time: 15 mins

Servings per Recipe: 4
Calories 350.4
Fat 13.2g
Cholesterol 95.6mg
Sodium 476.2mg
Carbohydrates 21.1g
Protein 36.6g

Ingredients

1/2 C. flour
1/4 C. cornmeal
1 tbsp Cajun seasoning
1/4 tsp salt
1/4 tsp ground black pepper
1/2 C. light mayonnaise

2 tbsp fresh dill, finely chopped
2 tbsp lemon juice
1 1/2 lbs tilapia fillets, cut in dices of 2 inches

Directions

1. Set your oven to 450 degrees F before doing anything else and grease a baking dish.
2. In a bowl, mix together the flour, cornmeal, Cajun seasoning, salt and pepper.
3. In another bowl, mix together the mayonnaise, dill and lemon juice.
4. Reserve 1/4 C. of the mayonnaise mixture in another bowl.
5. Dip the fish fillets in the mayonnaise mixture, then coat with the flour mixture.
6. Arrange the fish fillets onto the prepared baking sheet.
7. Cook in the oven for about 10 minutes.
8. Now, set the broiler of your oven.
9. Cook the croquettes under the broiler for about 4 minutes.
10. Serve with the reserved mayonnaise mixture.

Latin American Croquettes

Prep Time: 30 mins
Total Time: 1 hr 30 mins

Servings per Recipe: 2
Calories   503.3
Fat   25.8g
Cholesterol   227.3mg
Sodium   666.7mg
Carbohydrates   23.6g
Protein   42.0g

Ingredients

2 tbsp butter
1/4 C. onion, finely chopped
1/8 C. flour
1/4 tsp salt
1/8 tsp black pepper
1/2 C. milk
2 slices white bread, chopped fine
1/2 lb cooked chicken breast, chopped coarsely

flour
1 beaten egg
breadcrumbs
vegetable oil

Directions

1. In a pan, melt the butter and sauté the onion till ender.
2. Add the flour, salt and pepper and stir till well combined.
3. Slowly, add the milk and cook till the mixture becomes thick, stirring continuously.
4. Remove from the heat and stir in the bread and chicken.
5. Refrigerate to chill for about 1 hour.
6. Make 4 equal sized patties from the mixture.
7. Coat the patties with the flour and then dip in egg and finally coat with the breadcrumbs.
8. In a deep skillet, heat about 1/2-inch deep oil and fry the croquettes till browned from all sides.
9. Transfer the croquettes onto a paper towel lined plate to drain.

VEGETARIAN
Spicy Parsnip Croquettes

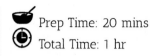

Prep Time: 20 mins
Total Time: 1 hr

Servings per Recipe: 6
Calories   231.9
Fat   9.8g
Cholesterol   82.3mg
Sodium   300.8mg
Carbohydrates   32.9g
Protein   4.7g

Ingredients

2 lbs parsnips, pared, cut into 2 inch lengths and fully cooked
1/2 tsp salt
2 eggs, well beaten
1/3 C. all-purpose flour
1 tbsp fresh minced parsley

1 jalapeno pepper, finely chopped (Optional)
pepper
1 pinch mace
4 -6 tbsp butter

Directions

1. In a food processor, add the parsnips and pulse till pureed with small lumps.
2. Transfer the parsnip puree in a bowl with eggs, flour, parsley, salt, pepper, mace and jalapeño and mix till well combined.
3. Refrigerate, covered for at least 1 hour.
4. Make about 3x1/2-inch thick patties from the mixture.
5. In a skillet, melt the butter and cook the croquettes for about 8 minutes per side.
6. Serve warm.

Croquettes Japanese Style

Prep Time: 30 mins
Total Time: 30 mins

Servings per Recipe: 1
Calories 231.9
Fat 2.8g
Cholesterol 33.1mg
Sodium 461.1mg
Carbohydrates 44.6g
Protein 7.3g

Ingredients

- 3 - 4 C. leftover mashed potatoes
- 1 C. corn
- 1/2 C. flour
- 1 egg, beaten
- 1 C. panko breadcrumbs
- oil (for frying)

Directions

1. In a bowl, mix together the mashed potatoes and corn.
2. Make flat patties from the mixture.
3. Coat the patties with the flour, then dip in beaten egg and finally with the panko.
4. In a deep skillet, heat the oil and fry the croquettes till browned from all sides.
5. Transfer the croquettes onto a paper towel lined plate to drain.
6. Serve alongside the Tonkatsu sauce.

SHRIMP and Rice Croquettes

Prep Time: 20 mins
Total Time: 28 mins

Servings per Recipe: 8
Calories   128.0
Fat   3.4g
Cholesterol   83.1mg
Sodium   36.7mg
Carbohydrates   19.4g
Protein   3.9g

Ingredients

1 C. uncooked rice
1 tbsp butter
2 eggs, slightly beaten
4 C. cooked shrimp, finely minced
cracker crumb
1 egg, beaten
oil (for frying)

Directions

1. In a pan of boiling water, cook the rice for about 20 minutes.
2. Drain completely and add immediately, stir in the butter.
3. Keep aside to cool slightly.
4. Stir in the shrimp, 2 eggs and seasoning.
5. Make cylinder shaped croquettes from the mixture.
6. Coat the croquettes in the cracker crumbs, then dip into beaten egg and finally, coat with the cracker crumbs again.
7. In a deep skillet, heat the oil to 375 degrees F and fry the croquettes till golden brown.

Tuscan Croquettes

Prep Time: 10 mins
Total Time: 20 mins

Servings per Recipe: 4
Calories   209.0
Fat   1.9g
Cholesterol   52.8mg
Sodium   29.4mg
Carbohydrates   36.9g
Protein   12.0g

Ingredients

2 C. drained cooked white beans, drained, reserving a few tbsp of liquid
1/2 C. onion, minced fine
1/4 C. fresh parsley, minced
1 egg, lightly beaten
salt
pepper
2 tbsp hot sauce
1/4 C. coarse cornmeal
peanut oil

Directions

1. Mash the beans roughly with a few lumps.
2. In a bowl, mix together the beans, onion, parsley, egg salt and pepper.
3. Slowly, add the cornmeal and mix till well combined.
4. Make hamburger shaped patties from the mixture.
5. Lightly, grease a pan with peanut oil and cook the patties for about 3-5 minutes per side.

MASHED POTATOES
Green Onions and Bacon Croquettes

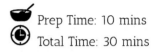

Prep Time: 10 mins
Total Time: 30 mins

Servings per Recipe:	8
Calories	223.1
Fat	4.8g
Cholesterol	9.3mg
Sodium	928.1mg
Carbohydrates	36.2g
Protein	8.3g

Ingredients

24 oz. prepared mashed potatoes
6 slices crumbled cooked turkey bacon
3 tbsp plain yogurt
1 chopped green onion

2 C. seasoned bread crumbs
1/4 tsp garlic salt
1/4 tsp white pepper

Directions

1. Set your oven to 400 degrees F before doing anything else.
2. In a bowl, add all the ingredients except 1 C. of the bread crumbs and mix till well combined.
3. Make 3/4-inch thick croquettes from the mixture.
4. Coat the croquettes with the remaining bread crumbs.
5. Arrange the croquettes into a non-stick baking dish.
6. Cook in the oven for about 20 minutes, flipping once in the middle way.

Mediterranean Mashed Potato Croquettes

Prep Time: 15 mins
Total Time: 25 mins

Servings per Recipe: 6
Calories   218.0
Fat   7.6g
Cholesterol   123.8mg
Sodium   454.3mg
Carbohydrates   27.9g
Protein   8.7g

Ingredients

2 C. leftover mashed potatoes
1/2 C. cooked arugula, squeezed of liquid and chopped
1/2 C. feta cheese, crumbled
2 garlic cloves, minced
1 pinch red pepper flakes
salt and pepper
1 egg
2 eggs, slightly beaten
1/8 C. cream
1/2 C. flour, seasoned with salt and pepper
1/2 C. breadcrumbs
vegetable oil, to fill pan by 3 inches (for frying)

Directions

1. In a bowl, add the mashed potatoes, cooked arugula, feta cheese, garlic, red pepper flakes salt, pepper and 1 egg and mix till well combined.
2. Make 20 golf sized balls from the mixture.
3. In a bowl, place the seasoned flour.
4. In another bowl, add 2 eggs and cream and beat well.
5. In a third bowl, place the breadcrumbs.
6. Coat the croquette with the flour, then dip in the egg mixture and finally, coat with the breadcrumbs.
7. In a deep skillet, heat the oil and deep fry the croquettes till browned from all sides.
8. Transfer the croquettes onto a paper towel lined plate to drain.
9. Sprinkle with the salt and pepper and serve.

COUNTRY HONEY Turkey and Swiss Croquettes

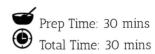

Prep Time: 30 mins
Total Time: 30 mins

Servings per Recipe: 4	
Calories	663.9
Fat	42.1g
Cholesterol	160.8mg
Sodium	552.1mg
Carbohydrates	24.4g
Protein	45.6g

Ingredients

- 1 lb ground turkey breast
- 1 celery rib, with leafy top finely chopped
- 1 large shallot, finely chopped
- 1/2 tsp ground thyme
- 1/2 tsp paprika
- 3 slices white bread, finely ground
- 1/2 C. milk
- 1 large egg
- 1/2 C. Parmigiano-Reggiano cheese
- 1/2 C. flat leaf parsley, finely chopped
- salt & freshly ground black pepper
- 4 slices honey-baked turkey
- 1/4 lb Swiss cheese, thinly sliced
- 1/2 C. dry breadcrumbs
- 1/2 C. olive oil

Directions

1. In a bowl, mix together the turkey, celery, thyme and paprika.
2. In a small bowl, mix together the ground bread and milk and then with your hands, squeeze the crumbs.
3. In the bowl, of turkey mixture, add the breadcrumbs, egg, Parmigiano-Reggiano and parsley, salt and pepper and mix till well combined.
4. Place a wax paper onto a smooth surface. With a rubber spatula, spread half of the turkey mixture over the wax paper into an 8-inch-square.
5. Top with the sliced turkey, followed by the Swiss cheese and remaining turkey mixture, forming the same square shape.
6. Seal the edges to secure the filling.
7. Cut into 4 square patties and coat with the bread crumbs.
8. In a large skillet, heat 1-inch olive oil on medium-high heat and fry the patties for about 10 minutes, turning once in the middle way.
9. Transfer the croquettes onto a paper towel lined plate to drain.
10. Sprinkle with the salt and serve.

Simply Italian
Cheese Croquettes

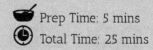

Prep Time: 5 mins
Total Time: 25 mins

Servings per Recipe: 4
Calories   741.7
Fat   29.4g
Cholesterol   195.6mg
Sodium   850.5mg
Carbohydrates   77.4g
Protein   38.9g

Ingredients

340 g flour
2 eggs
455 g mozzarella cheese
salt
pepper
55 g breadcrumbs

oil (for frying)

Directions

1. In a bowl, mix together the flour, salt and pepper.
2. Make a well in the center of the flour mixture.
3. Add the eggs in the middle of the flour mixture.
4. Add the mozzarella and mix till well combined.
5. Make croquettes from the mixture.
6. Coat the croquettes in the breadcrumbs evenly.
7. In a deep skillet, heat the oil and deep fry the croquettes till browned from all sides.
8. Transfer the croquettes onto a paper towel lined plate to drain.

FIESTA
Croquettes

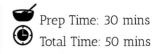
Prep Time: 30 mins
Total Time: 50 mins

Servings per Recipe: 6
Calories 657.7
Fat 39.2g
Cholesterol 101.9mg
Sodium 1039.4mg
Carbohydrates 60.4g
Protein 18.4g

Ingredients

- 3/4 C. parmesan cheese
- 3/4 C. breadcrumbs
- 3/4 C. panko breadcrumbs
- 1 (1 oz.) packet Hidden Valley Original Ranch Dips Mix
- 2 eggs, slightly beaten
- 1/2 C. Hidden Valley® Original Ranch® Dressing
- 3 C. butternut squash, chopped into 3/4-inch chunks
- 4 C. bibb lettuce, torn into bite-sized pieces
- 4 C. baby spinach leaves, loosely packed
- 1 Fuji apple, diced into 1/2-inch pieces
- 1 bosc pear, diced into 1/2-inch pieces
- 6 slices turkey bacon, crisp cooked and crumbled
- 1 C. gorgonzola, crumbled
- 1/3 C. balsamic vinegar
- 1 (1 oz.) packet Hidden Valley® Original Ranch® Dressing and Seasoning Mix
- 1/3 C. olive oil
- 1/2 C. pure maple syrup
- 1/2 C. plain Greek yogurt

Directions

1. Set your oven to 325 degrees F before doing anything else and generously, grease a baking sheet.
2. In a bowl, mix together the Parmesan cheese, bread crumbs, panko bread crumbs and packet of Hidden Valley® Original Ranch® Dips.
3. In another bowl mix beaten eggs and 1/2 C. of the Hidden Valley® Original Ranch® dressing.
4. Dip the squash chunks into the egg-dressing liquid and then coat with the bread crumb mixture evenly.
5. Arrange the squash chunks onto the prepared baking sheet.
6. Refrigerate to chill for about 10-15 minutes.
7. Cook in the oven for about 20 minutes, flipping once in the middle way.

8. In a large platter, arrange the lettuce and spinach and top with the apples, pears, bacon, and Gorgonzola.
9. For the dressing in a medium pan, add the balsamic vinegar and 1 packet Hidden Valley® The Original Ranch® Salad Dressing Mix and beat well.
10. Slowly, add the olive oil and maple syrup, beating continuously.
11. Add the yogurt and cook on medium-low heat till heated completely.
12. Arrange the squash croquettes over the salad and drizzle with the warm dressing.
13. Serve immediately.

CHEDDAR Halibut Croquettes

Prep Time: 20 mins
Total Time: 50 mins

Servings per Recipe: 6
Calories   171.1
Fat   12.2g
Cholesterol   100.4mg
Sodium   621.0mg
Carbohydrates   7.2g
Protein   8.0g

Ingredients

- 2 C. cooked halibut, flaked
- 1 C. grated sharp cheddar cheese
- 2 eggs, well beaten
- 1 tsp salt
- 1/2 C. dried breadcrumbs
- 2 tbsp butter, melted
- 2 tbsp lemon juice

Directions

1. Set your oven to 350 degrees F before doing anything else and grease a baking dish.
2. In a pan of boiling water, add the halibut and cook till it just rises on the top.
3. Drain the halibut and with a fork, flake it.
4. In a bowl, mix together the cooked halibut ingredients except the bread crumbs and lemon juice.
5. Make 6 equal sized croquettes from the mixture.
6. Coat the croquettes with bread crumbs evenly and arrange onto the prepared baking dish.
7. Cook in the oven for about 25-30 minutes.
8. Serve with a drizzling of the lemon juice.

Croquettes Asian Style

Prep Time: 15 mins
Total Time: 40 mins

Servings per Recipe: 8
Calories 238.3
Fat 6.2g
Cholesterol 28.3mg
Sodium 500.6mg
Carbohydrates 38.8g
Protein 8.0g

Ingredients

- 2 C. rotisserie chicken
- 1 (8 oz.) cans water chestnuts
- 1 (10 oz.) cans bamboo shoots
- 1 C. celery
- 3 green onions
- 1/4 C. mayonnaise
- 1/4 C. Miracle Whip
- 3 tbsp reduced soy sauce
- 1 tbsp ginger
- 1/2 tbsp sesame oil
- 2 tbsp lemon juice
- 2 tbsp rice vinegar
- 1 C. quick-cooking oats
- 2 C. panko breadcrumbs
- 1 egg

Directions

1. Set your oven to 400 degrees F before doing anything else and grease a baking sheet.
2. Chop all the vegetables finely and shred the chicken.
3. In a bowl, add all the vegetables, shredded chicken and remaining ingredients except the panko.
4. Make the croquettes from the mixture.
5. Coat the croquettes with bread crumbs evenly and arrange onto the prepared baking sheet.
6. Cook in the oven for about 22 minutes, flipping once after 10 minutes.

TURKEY, MUSHROOMS, and Spice Croquettes

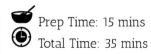

Prep Time: 15 mins
Total Time: 35 mins

Servings per Recipe: 8
Calories 319.7
Fat 18.5g
Cholesterol 69.3mg
Sodium 699.5mg
Carbohydrates 22.0g
Protein 16.2g

Ingredients

1 garlic clove, cracked from skin
1/2 small onion
1 celery rib, chopped
1/4 small red bell pepper, chopped
1 C. chopped cooked turkey, white and dark
1 C. leftover mashed potatoes
1 egg
salt and pepper
2 tsp poultry seasoning
3 sprigs parsley, leaves only

1 C. Italian seasoned breadcrumbs
3 tbsp butter
4 tbsp extra virgin olive oil
12 cremini mushrooms, thinly sliced
3 - 4 sprigs fresh rosemary, finely chopped
2 tbsp all-purpose flour
3 C. chicken stock
1/2 C. grated Romano cheese

Directions

1. In a food processor, add the garlic, onion, celery and red bell pepper and pulse till chopped finely.
2. Add the turkey, potatoes, egg, salt, pepper, poultry seasoning and parsley leaves and pulse till well combined.
3. Transfer the turkey mixture into a bowl with 3/4 C. of the bread crumbs and mix well.
4. In a small skillet, melt 2 tbsp of butter and 1 tbsp of the oil on medium heat and cook the mushrooms for about 5-6 minutes.
5. Stir in the salt, pepper, rosemary and flour and cook for about 1 minute.
6. Stir in the stock and bring to a boil.
7. Reduce the heat to medium-low heat and cook for about 5 minutes.
8. Make 8 equal sized croquettes from the mixture.
9. In a shallow dish, mix together the cheese and remaining 1/4 C. of the bread crumbs.
10. Coat the croquettes with the cheese mixture evenly.

11. In a nonstick skillet, heat 3 tbsp of the extra-virgin olive oil on medium heat and cook the croquettes in batches for about 5-6 minutes.
12. Transfer the croquettes onto a paper towel lined plate to drain.
13. Pour the rosemary gravy over the croquettes and serve.

ROASTED RED PEPPER and Chickpea Croquettes

Prep Time: 15 mins
Total Time: 45 mins

Servings per Recipe: 8
Calories 217.2
Fat 9.9g
Cholesterol 30.4mg
Sodium 400.9mg
Carbohydrates 27.2g
Protein 9.9g

Ingredients

1 C. plain yogurt
1/4 C. chopped of fresh mint
1 garlic clove, chopped
1 (19 oz.) can chickpeas, drained
1 onion, finely chopped
4 tsp hot curry paste
1 egg, beaten
1/2 C. store bought roasted red pepper, chopped
3/4 C. oat bran
3/4 C. finely chopped almonds
salt and pepper

Directions

1. In a small bowl, mix together the yogurt, mint and garlic and refrigerate, covered for about 30 minutes.
2. Stir in the salt and pepper.
3. Set your oven to 375 degrees F before doing anything else and line a baking sheet with the parchment paper.
4. In a large bowl, add the chickpeas, onion, curry paste and egg and with a potato masher, mash till just combined but not smooth.
5. Add the red peppers, oat bran, salt and pepper and with a fork, mix till well combined.
6. Make 8 equal sized patties from the mixture.
7. Coat the patties with the chopped almonds and arrange onto the prepared baking sheet.
8. Cook in the oven for about 30 minutes, flipping once in the middle way.
9. Arrange the croquette over the bed of salad greens and serve alongside the yogurt sauce.

Fall-Time Pumpkin Croquettes

Prep Time: 1 hr
Total Time: 1 hr 5 mins

Servings per Recipe: 20
Calories 21.6
Fat 1.6g
Cholesterol 23.4mg
Sodium 25.4mg
Carbohydrates 0.2g
Protein 1.5g

Ingredients

1 small butternut pumpkin, cut in 1/2 and seeds removed
1 tsp grated nutmeg
sea salt
fresh ground black pepper
100 g soft fresh goat cheese
1 tbsp chopped sage
1 tbsp champagne vinegar
plain flour, for dusting
2 eggs, beaten
dried breadcrumbs, for coating
oil, for deep frying

Directions

1. Set your oven to 350 degrees F before doing anything else.
2. Arrange the pumpkin on a baking dish and cook in the oven for about 45 minutes.
3. Remove from the oven and keep aside to cool.
4. Peel the pumpkin and chop the flesh.
5. In a food processor, add the pumpkin flesh, nutmeg and salt and pulse till smooth.
6. In a bowl, mix together the goat cheese, sage, vinegar and salt.
7. Make small marble sized balls from the mixture.
8. Dip the croquettes with the pumpkin puree mixture evenly, then coat with the flour.
9. Now, dip in the beaten egg and finally, coat with the breadcrumbs evenly.
10. In a large frying pan, heat the enough oil and deep fry the croquettes for about 3 minutes.
11. Transfer the croquettes onto a paper towel lined plate to drain.
12. Serve warm.

IRISH DINNER
Croquettes

 Prep Time: 15 mins
 Total Time: 20 mins

Servings per Recipe: 8
Calories   49.8
Fat   1.4g
Cholesterol   53.4mg
Sodium   21.8mg
Carbohydrates   6.8g
Protein   2.4g

Ingredients

2 C. mashed potatoes, left overs are fine
seasoned with
salt, to taste, and
pepper, to taste
3 C. finely chopped corned beef
1 egg
1 tbsp finely chopped parsley

1 egg
2 tbsp milk
dried breadcrumbs

Directions

1. In a bowl, add the potatoes, corned beef, egg and seasoning and mix well.
2. Make the croquettes from the mixture.
3. In a shallow dish, mix together the egg and milk.
4. In another shallow dish, place the breadcrumbs.
5. Dip the croquettes into the egg mixture and then coat with the breadcrumbs.
6. In a skillet, heat the oil to 375 degrees F and fry the croquettes till golden brown.

Cheddar and Aubergine Croquettes

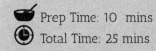

Prep Time: 10 mins
Total Time: 25 mins

Servings per Recipe: 4
Calories   814.0
Fat   68.8g
Cholesterol   136.8mg
Sodium   1343.8mg
Carbohydrates   35.6g
Protein   17.4g

Ingredients

- 2 eggplants, peeled and cubed
- 1 C. grated sharp cheddar cheese
- 1 tbsp grated Parmesan cheese
- 1 C. Italian seasoned breadcrumbs
- 2 large eggs
- 2 tbsp chopped fresh basil
- 3 tbsp minced yellow onions
- 2 garlic cloves, minced
- 1 C. vegetable oil
- 1 tsp salt, to taste
- 1/2 tsp fresh ground black pepper

Directions

1. In a pan, add the eggplant in a small amount of boiling water and cook, covered for about 4-5 minutes.
2. Drain the eggplants and transfer into a bowl.
3. With a fork, mash well.
4. Add the remaining ingredients except oil and mix till well combined.
5. Make the patties from the mixture.
6. In a skillet, heat the oil and fry the croquettes for about 5 minutes per side.

MEXICAN
Croquettes

Prep Time: 20 mins
Total Time: 40 mins

Servings per Recipe: 4
Calories 436.5
Fat 13.1g
Cholesterol 0.0mg
Sodium 280.9mg
Carbohydrates 65.8g
Protein 19.1g

Ingredients

2 (15 oz.) cans black beans, rinsed
1 tsp ground cumin
1 C. frozen corn kernels, thawed
1/4 C. plain breadcrumbs, plus
1/3 C. plain breadcrumbs, divided
2 C. finely chopped tomatoes
2 scallions, sliced
1/4 C. chopped fresh cilantro
1 tsp chili powder, divided
1/4 tsp salt
1 tbsp extra virgin olive oil
1 avocado, diced

Directions

1. Set your oven to 425 degrees F before doing anything else and grease a baking sheet.
2. In a large bowl, add the black beans and cumin and with a fork, mash well.
3. Add the corn and 1/4 C. of the breadcrumbs and mix well.
4. In another bowl, mix together the tomatoes, scallions, cilantro, 1/2 tsp of the chili powder and salt.
5. Add 1 C. of the tomato mixture into the beans mixture and mix well.
6. In a small bowl, mix together the remaining 1/3 C. breadcrumbs, oil and the remaining 1/2 tsp of the chili powder.
7. Divide the bean mixture into 8 equal sized balls.
8. Coat the balls with the breadcrumb mixture evenly and arrange onto the prepared baking sheet.
9. Cook in the oven for about 20 minutes.
10. Add the avocado into the remaining tomato mixture and mix.
11. Serve the croquettes with the salsa.

European Veal Croquettes

Prep Time: 30 mins
Total Time: 1 hr

Servings per Recipe: 4
Calories 960.0
Fat 39.6g
Cholesterol 338.1mg
Sodium 1094.8mg
Carbohydrates 88.5g
Protein 53.4g

Ingredients

600 g fresh veal
salt and pepper
75 g butter
1 tbsp vegetable oil
1/2 C. white wine
1 small onion, finely chopped
1 clove garlic
2 bay leaves
1/4 tsp ground nutmeg
2 sprigs parsley, finely chopped

3/4 tsp thyme
2 tsp lemon zest
2 C. water
40 g all-purpose flour
cornstarch
3 eggs, separated into yolks and whites
4 C. fine breadcrumbs
vegetable oil, to deep-fry

Directions

1. Season the veal with the salt and pepper.
2. In a large pan melt 2 tbsp of the butter on medium-high heat.
3. Add the veal, wine, onion, garlic, bay leaves, nutmeg, parsley, thyme, lemon zest and water and bring to a boil.
4. Reduce the heat and simmer for about 45-60 minutes.
5. Strain the stock into a bowl and reserve.
6. Chop the veal finely.
7. In a pan, melt the remaining butter on low heat.
8. Add the flour and cook, stirring for a few minutes.
9. Increase the heat to medium.
10. Slowly, add the stock and cook till the sauce becomes smooth and thick, stirring continuously.
11. Remove from the heat and keep aside to cool slightly.
12. Add 3 egg yolks and mix well.

13. Add the cooked veal, salt and pepper and mix till a thick and stiff mixture forms.
14. Keep the mixture aside to cool completely.
15. Cut the mixture into 1 1/2x3-inch rolls.
16. Spread the crumbs on a clean, dry cutting board.
17. In a shallow, dish beat the egg whites slightly.
18. Coat the croquettes with the breadcrumbs, then dip in the egg whites and coat with the breadcrumbs evenly.
19. In a skillet, heat the oil and deep fry the croquettes in batches for about 4 minutes.
20. Transfer the croquettes onto a paper towel lined plate to drain.
21. Serve hot alongside the French fries.

Pinto Beans and Carrot Croquettes

Prep Time: 15 mins
Total Time: 30 mins

Servings per Recipe: 3
Calories	181.7
Fat	1.7g
Cholesterol	0.0mg
Sodium	412.2mg
Carbohydrates	35.0g
Protein	7.2g

Ingredients

- 1 medium onion, diced
- 1 C. canned pinto beans, mashed
- 1 1/2 C. raw carrots, grated
- 1/2 C. fresh breadcrumb
- 1/4 tsp dried sage
- salt and pepper

Directions

1. Set your oven to 375 degrees F before doing anything else.
2. In a bowl, add all the ingredients and mix well.
3. Make about 1 1/2-inch balls from the mixture and arrange onto an ungreased cookie sheet.
4. Cook in the oven for about 15-20 minutes.
5. Serve alongside your favorite sauce.

ZUCCHINI CROQUETTES Southern Greek Style

Prep Time: 25 mins
Total Time: 48 mins

Servings per Recipe: 1
Calories	17.8
Fat	0.7g
Cholesterol	8.6mg
Sodium	156.6mg
Carbohydrates	2.1g
Protein	0.7g

Ingredients

- 1 1/4 lbs zucchini, thinly grated
- 1 large white onion, grated
- 1 1/2 tsp kosher salt
- 3 tbsp fresh dill, snipped
- 3 tbsp of fresh mint, snipped
- 1 large egg, beaten
- 1/3 C. grated pecorino cheese
- 1/4 C. breadcrumbs
- 1 tbsp butter, melted
- olive oil (for frying)

Directions

1. In a colander, place the zucchini and onions and sprinkle with the salt.
2. Keep aside for about 20 minutes.
3. Squeeze out all the water from the zucchini mixture and transfer into a bowl.
4. Add the dill, mint, egg, cheese, bread crumbs and butter and mix well.
5. Make small sized balls from the mixture.
6. In a deep skillet, heat about 5 1/2-inch olive oil to 325 degrees F and deep fry the croquettes for about 2-3 minutes.
7. Transfer the croquettes onto a paper towel lined plate to drain.
8. Serve hot.

New England Curry Crab Croquettes

Prep Time: 20 mins
Total Time: 35 mins

Servings per Recipe: 6
Calories   212.8
Fat   7.6g
Cholesterol   134.4mg
Sodium   615.1mg
Carbohydrates   14.7g
Protein   21.3g

Ingredients

1 lb flaked crab
2 eggs
1/4 C. flour
1 tbsp soy sauce
3 stalks celery
1 medium onion
1 tsp paprika
salt and pepper
oil (for frying)

DIPPING SAUCE
1/2 lb fresh ricotta cheese
1 (15 oz.) cans crushed tomatoes
1 tsp curry powder
2 tsp brown sugar

Directions

1. For the dipping sauce in a bowl, mix together all the ingredients and refrigerate for about 30 minutes.
2. In a food processor, add the celery stalks and onion and pulse till finely minced.
3. Add the crab, eggs, flour, soy sauce, paprika and salt and pepper and pulse till a thick paste is formed.
4. Make croquettes from the mixture.
5. In a frying pan, heat the oil and shallow fry the croquettes for about 8-10 minutes.
6. Serve the croquettes warm alongside the dipping sauce.

RUSTIC SPANISH
Croquettes

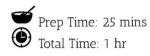
Prep Time: 25 mins
Total Time: 1 hr

Servings per Recipe: 16
Calories 64.3
Fat 4.8g
Cholesterol 31.9mg
Sodium 144.2mg
Carbohydrates 1.5g
Protein 3.4g

Ingredients

14 oz. beef
3 chorizo sausage, slices, optional
pepper (to taste)
nutmeg (to taste)
oregano (to taste)
olive oil
1 medium onion
4 garlic cloves
1 egg yolk

1 egg
breadcrumbs
1 tbsp all-purpose flour
parsley (to taste)
salt (to taste)
vegetable oil (for frying)

Directions

1. Cut the beef into pieces.
2. In a food processor, add the meat, chorizo slices and the oregano and pulse till chopped slightly.
3. Transfer the meat mixture into a bowl with the salt, pepper and nutmeg and with your hands, mix well.
4. In a pan, heat the olive oil on low heat and sauté the chopped onion and chopped garlic just begins to turn golden brown.
5. Stir in the meat mixture and simmer for about 15-20 minutes, stirring occasionally.
6. Remove from the heat and add the egg yolk and mix well.
7. Stir in the flour and return the pan on the stove and cook for about 3-4 minutes.
8. Remove from the heat and top with the chopped parsley.
9. Keep aside to cool in the room temperature.
10. Make small sized croquette from the mixture.
11. In a bowl, add the eggs and beat well.
12. Coat the croquettes with the breadcrumbs, then dip in the eggs mixture and finally, coat

with the breadcrumbs again.
13. In a skillet, heat the oil and fry the croquettes till golden.
14. Transfer the croquettes onto a paper towel lined plate to drain.
15. Serve the croquettes alongside the rice and salad.

FRENCH
Spinach Croquettes

Prep Time: 30 mins
Total Time: 39 mins

Servings per Recipe: 1
Calories 98.1
Fat 5.2g
Cholesterol 48.9mg
Sodium 203.0mg
Carbohydrates 7.7g
Protein 5.7g

Ingredients

2 lbs fresh spinach, trimmed and washed
1 medium onion, chopped
3 eggs, lightly beaten
1 C. grated gruyere cheese
1 C. breadcrumbs
1/2 tsp salt
1/4 tsp black pepper
1 tbsp extra virgin olive oil
1 tbsp unsalted butter

Directions

1. In a large pan of lightly salted boiling water, cook the spinach and onion for about 1 minute.
2. Drain well and keep aside. To cool slightly.
3. Squeeze the spinach and onion and then chop them.
4. In a large bowl, add the spinach mixture, eggs, cheese, breadcrumbs, salt and pepper and mix well.
5. Make 16 small sized croquettes from the mixture and keep aside for about 5-10 minutes.
6. In a large nonstick skillet, heat the oil and butter on medium-high heat and fry the croquettes in batches for about 3-4 minutes per side.
7. Serve hot.

Mustard Curry Ground Beef Croquettes with Sauce

Prep Time: 20 mins
Total Time: 40 mins

Servings per Recipe: 5
Calories   444.5
Fat   28.6g
Cholesterol   138.6mg
Sodium   449.4mg
Carbohydrates   21.8g
Protein   24.1g

Ingredients

CROQUETTES
3 tbsp butter
1/4-1/2 tsp curry powder
1/4 C. all-purpose flour
1/4 C. milk
2 tsp prepared mustard
1 tsp grated onion
2 C. coarsely ground cooked beef
2/3 C. fine dry breadcrumb
1 beaten egg
2 tbsp water

cooking oil, for deep-fat frying
CHEESE SAUCE
2 tbsp butter
2 tbsp flour
1/4 tsp salt
1/8 tsp pepper
1 1/4 C. milk
1/2 C. shredded American cheese
1/2 C. shredded Swiss cheese

Directions

1. In a pan, melt the butter and stir in the curry powder and flour.
2. Add the milk and cook for about 2 minutes, stirring continuously.
3. Remove from the heat and stir in the onion, mustard and ground beef.
4. Refrigerate, covered for about 1 hour.
5. With wet hands, make 10 balls from the mixture.
6. In a shallow dish, place the breadcrumbs.
7. In another shallow dish, beat together the egg and water.
8. Coat the balls with the bread crumbs and then shape into a cone.
9. Dip the cons into the egg mixture and coat with the breadcrumbs again.
10. In a skillet, heat the oil and fry the croquettes in batches for about 2-2 1/2 minutes.
11. Transfer the croquettes onto a paper towel lined plate to drain.
12. For the sauce in a small pan, melt the butter and stir in the flour, salt and pepper.

13. Add the milk and cook for about 2 minutes.
14. Add the cheeses and cook till melted completely.
15. Serve the croquettes alongside the cheese sauce.

Southern Black-Eyed Pea Croquettes

Prep Time: 10 mins
Total Time: 17 mins

Servings per Recipe: 6
Calories   183.2
Fat   2.5g
Cholesterol   62.0mg
Sodium   581.2mg
Carbohydrates   30.3g
Protein   10.2g

Ingredients

2 (15 oz.) cans black-eyed peas, drained and rinsed
2 eggs, lightly beaten
1 C. finely chopped onion
1/2 C. finely chopped bell pepper
1/2 C. self-rising flour
1/4 tsp pepper
2 tsp season salt

Directions

1. In large bowl, add the black-eyed peas and mash slightly.
2. Add the remaining ingredients, except oil and mix till well combined.
3. With 1/4 C. of the mixture, make slightly flatten croquettes.
4. In a large deep skillet, heat the oil on medium-high heat and cook the croquets in batches for about 7 minutes, flipping once in the middle way.
5. Transfer the croquettes onto a paper towel lined plate to drain.

OCTOBER'S TURKEY and Celery Croquettes

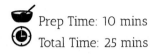

Prep Time: 10 mins
Total Time: 25 mins

Servings per Recipe: 4
Calories   411.3
Fat   16.0g
Cholesterol   107.1mg
Sodium   420.5mg
Carbohydrates   36.1g
Protein   28.8g

Ingredients

2 C. cooked turkey, finely chopped
1 3/4 C. panko breadcrumbs, divided
2 tbsp milk
1 1/2 tsp sage
salt and pepper
1 egg
1/2 chopped onion
1/2 stalk celery, chopped
2 1/2 tbsp oil, divided

Directions

1. Heat a skillet with a drop of oil and sauté the onion till tender.
2. Remove from the heat and keep aside to cool slightly.
3. Transfer the onion into a bowl with the turkey, 1/4 C. of the panko, milk, sage, egg, salt and pepper and mix well.
4. Refrigerate for at least 30 minutes.
5. Make 12 patties from the mixture.
6. Coat the patties with the remaining panko evenly.
7. In a large frying pan, heat the oil and fry the patties in batches for about 3-5 minutes per side.
8. Serve alongside the cranberry sauce.

Minced Mushroom and Rice Croquettes

Prep Time: 15 mins
Total Time: 30 mins

Servings per Recipe: 4
Calories   717.5
Cholesterol   15.2g
Sodium   154.3mg
Carbohydrates   835.6mg
Protein   119.2g

Ingredients

RICE MIXTURE
1/4 C. chopped onion
1 tbsp oil
1 C. minced mushroom
2 C. cooked rice
3 tbsp minced celery
2 tbsp minced green bell peppers
1 tbsp grated carrot
1/2 C. cheddar cheese
1 tbsp minced fresh parsley (optional)
1 tsp paprika
1/2 tsp salt
1/4 tsp black pepper (optional)
2 tsp lemon juice
1 egg
ROLLING MIXTURE
2 C. fresh breadcrumbs
2 eggs
oil (for frying)

Directions

1. In a large skillet, heat the oil and sauté the onion and mushroom till tender.
2. Transfer the onion mixture into a bowl with remaining ingredients and mix well.
3. Refrigerate to chill the mixture before serving.
4. In a shallow dish, beat the eggs.
5. In another shallow dish, place the breadcrumbs.
6. Make croquettes from the mixture.
7. Dip the croquettes in eggs and then coat with breadcrumbs evenly.
8. In a deep skillet, heat the oil and fry the croquettes in batches till golden browned evenly.

CORNED BEEF and Sauerkraut Croquettes

Prep Time: 25 mins
Total Time: 30 mins

Servings per Recipe: 6
Calories   430.4
Fat   19.9g
Cholesterol   177.8mg
Sodium   1823.8mg
Carbohydrates   37.5g
Protein   23.9g

Ingredients

1/2 C. converted rice
1 (16 oz.) cans sauerkraut
1 (12 oz.) cans corned beef
1/4 C. chopped onion
3 eggs
1 C. shredded Swiss cheese
1 tsp salt
1/4 tsp pepper
2 tbsp water
1 1/2 C. fine dry breadcrumbs

Directions

1. Cook the rice according to package's instructions.
2. Drain sauerkraut very well and chop finely alongside the corned beef.
3. In a bowl, add the sauerkraut, corned beef, onion, 2 eggs, rice, cheese, salt and pepper and mix well.
4. With about 1/4 C. of the mixture, make 18 equal sized croquettes.
5. In a shallow dish, beat the remaining egg and water.
6. Coat the croquettes with the bread crumbs, then dip in the egg mixture and finally, coat with the breadcrumbs again.
7. Keep aside for at least 10 minutes.
8. In a deep skillet, heat the oil and shallow fry the croquettes in batches for about 5-7 minutes, flipping once.
9. Serve alongside the Thousand Island dressing.

Nutmeg Croquettes

Prep Time: 15 mins
Total Time: 35 mins

Servings per Recipe: 4
Calories 866.5
Fat 53.2g
Cholesterol 394.3mg
Sodium 587.6mg
Carbohydrates 51.5g
Protein 44.4g

Ingredients

4 tbsp butter
1/3 C. flour
1 1/2 C. milk
1/4 tsp pepper
1/4 tsp nutmeg
3 egg yolks
4 C. Swiss cheese, shredded

2 eggs
1/2 C. milk
1/2 C. flour
1 C. fine dry breadcrumb
oil

Directions

1. In a medium pan, melt the butter and stir in 1/3 C. of the flour till well combined.
2. Add 1 1/2 C. of the milk and cook till thick, stirring continuously.
3. Stir in the pepper and nutmeg.
4. Stir about 1/2 C. of the hot mixture into egg yolks.
5. Return the egg yolk mixture to hot mixture and mix well.
6. Cook for about 10 minutes, stirring continuously.
7. Add thee cheese and stir till smooth.
8. Place the cheese mixture in lightly greased 11x7x1 1/2-inch baking dish.
9. Refrigerate to chill till firm.
10. Cut chilled mixture into 12 equal sized portions.
11. In small bowl, beat together 2 eggs and 1/2 C. of the milk.
12. Coat the croquettes with 1/2 C. of the flour, then dip in egg mixture and finally, coat with the breadcrumb.
13. In a deep skillet, heat the oil to 375 degrees F and deep fry the croquettes for about 2-3 minutes.
14. Transfer the croquettes onto a paper towel lined plate to drain.

CRANBERRY
Croquettes

Prep Time: 30 mins
Total Time: 45 mins

Servings per Recipe: 12
Calories 97.6
Fat 0.6g
Cholesterol 17.9mg
Sodium 165.2mg
Carbohydrates 21.6g
Protein 1.7g

Ingredients

1 C. flour
2 tsp baking powder
1/2 tsp salt
1 egg
2 tbsp milk
1/2 tbsp lemon juice
2 tsp orange zest

3/4 C. grated cranberries, cooked in simple syrup and drained save syrup
SIMPLE SYRUP
1 C. water
3/4 C. sugar

Directions

1. In a bowl, mix together the flour, baking powder and salt.
2. In another bowl, beat together the egg and milk.
3. Add the egg mixture into flour mixture and mix well.
4. Stir in the berries and lemon juice.
5. Make small sized flattened croquettes from the mixture.
6. In a deep skillet, heat about 1/2-inch of the oil and fry the croquettes till crispy from both sides.
7. Transfer the croquettes onto a paper towel lined plate to drain.
8. Sprinkle with the sugar and serve alongside the warm syrup from cooking the berries.

Spicy Leftover Rice Croquettes

Prep Time: 2 mins
Total Time: 2 mins

Servings per Recipe: 4
Calories	248.0
Fat	8.8g
Cholesterol	123.2mg
Sodium	114.2mg
Carbohydrates	32.2g
Protein	8.8g

Ingredients

- 1 1/2 C. cooked rice, cooled
- 1/2 C. all-purpose flour
- 1 tbsp butter, softened
- 2 eggs, well beaten
- 1/3 C. grated sharp cheddar cheese
- 1/4 tsp cayenne pepper
- salt
- fresh breadcrumb

Directions

1. In a bowl, mix together the rice, flour, and butter.
2. Add the eggs, cheese, Cayenne and salt and mix well.
3. Make equal sized balls from the mixture.
4. Coat the balls with the breadcrumbs evenly.
5. In a deep skillet, heat the oil and deep fry the croquettes for about 2 minutes.
6. Transfer the croquettes onto a paper towel lined plate to drain.
7. Serve immediately.

WILD GAME
Croquettes

Prep Time: 1 hr
Total Time: 1 hr

Servings per Recipe: 4
Calories	798.2
Fat	40.9g
Cholesterol	286.9mg
Sodium	676.8mg
Carbohydrates	68.0g
Protein	38.1g

Ingredients

12 oz. pheasant breast, cut into 1/2 pieces
4 oz. heavy cream
1 tbsp chopped sage
1 tbsp chopped oregano
2 tbsp butter
2 tbsp flour
1 C. milk
salt
1 C. flour
3 eggs, whipped
1 1/2 C. panko breadcrumbs
fry oil (1 quart for frying)
CURRY DIPPING SAUCE
1/2 C. mayonnaise
1/4 C. sour cream
1 tbsp red curry paste
1 tbsp cider vinegar

Directions

1. In a food processor, add the pheasant and pulse till smooth.
2. While the motor is running, slowly, add the cream.
3. Add the herbs and a pinch of salt and pulse till combined.
4. Transfer the mixture into a bowl and refrigerate till serving.
5. For the béchamel in a small pan, melt the butter and stir in the flour and beat till a paste forms.
6. Add a little milk and beat till smooth.
7. Slowly, add the remaining milk, beating continuously and bring to a simmer.
8. Season with the salt and keep aside to cool.
9. Add the milk mixture in the bowl with the chucker puree and refrigerate to keep cold.
10. For the croquettes line a small sheet pan with wax paper.
11. With 2 tsp of the mixture, make three-sided football shaped balls.
12. Arrange the balls onto wax paper lined sheet pan and freeze for at least 15 minutes.

13. In a shallow dish, place the flour.
14. In a second shallow dish, beat the eggs.
15. In a third shallow dish, place the breadcrumbs.
16. Coat the croquettes with the flour, then dip in the egg and finally coat with the breadcrumbs.
17. In a fryer, heat the oil to 360 degrees F and fry the croquette for about 3 minutes.
18. Serve hot alongside the curry dipping sauce.
19. For the curry dipping sauce in a bowl, mix together all the ingredients.

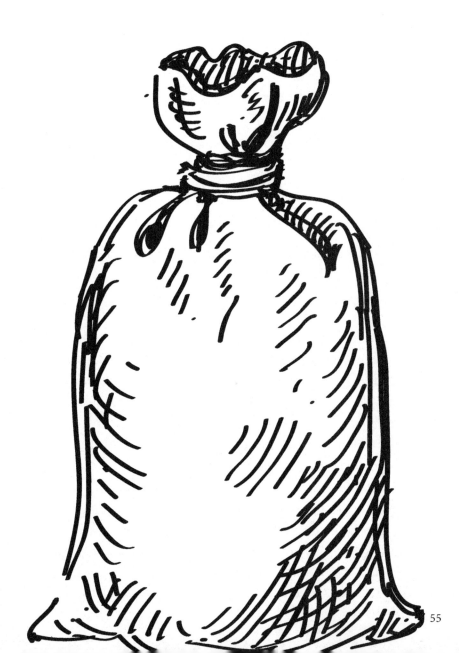

ENGLISH CHEESE Croquettes

Prep Time: 1 hr 20 mins
Total Time: 1 hr 30 mins

Servings per Recipe: 4
Calories 741.2
Fat 47.8g
Cholesterol 189.7mg
Sodium 988.6mg
Carbohydrates 51.2g
Protein 26.1g

Ingredients

250 g camembert cheese, chilled
1/4 C. fresh basil
1/4 C. unsalted butter
6 tbsp flour, divided
1 C. milk
1 pinch nutmeg
2 eggs
2 C. breadcrumbs
1/4 C. olive oil
salt and pepper

Directions

1. Cut the rind from the cheese and chop into small chunks.
2. Chop the basil finely.
3. For the béchamel in a heavy medium pan, melt the butter on medium heat and cook 4 tbsp of the flour, for about 2 minutes, beating continuously.
4. Add the milk and cook for about 3-4 minutes, beating continuously.
5. Add the nutmeg, cheese and basil and stir till the cheese melts.
6. Remove from the heat and stir in the salt and pepper.
7. Add 1 egg and stir to combine. In a large pie plate, place the mixture and keep aside.
8. Press a plastic wrap over the surface of the mixture and refrigerate to chill for overnight.
9. Make walnut-sized balls from the mix and dust with a little flour.
10. Refrigerate to chill for about 1 hour.
11. In a shallow dish, beat the remaining egg.
12. Slightly, press the cheese balls into 3/4-inch thickness.
13. Dip the croquettes into the egg and then coat with the bread crumbs evenly.
14. In a large, heavy-bottomed skillet, heat the oil on medium heat and fry the croquettes in batches for about 1 minute per side.
15. Transfer the croquettes onto a paper towel lined plate to drain. Serve warm.

Tomato and Ricotta Italian Croquettes

Prep Time: 20 mins
Total Time: 1 hr

Servings per Recipe: 4
Calories 1386.9
Fat 124.1g
Cholesterol 237.7mg
Sodium 307.8mg
Carbohydrates 50.6g
Protein 20.5g

Ingredients

- 16 oz. ripe tomatoes
- 10 oz. ricotta cheese, drained and crumbled
- 2 eggs, beaten until foamy, plus 2 egg yolks
- 2 tbsp finely chopped parsley
- 1/4 tsp freshly grated nutmeg
- salt & freshly ground black pepper
- 1 C. all-purpose flour
- 1 C. fine dry breadcrumb
- 2 C. olive oil, for frying

Directions

1. In a pan of boiling water, blanch the tomatoes for about 1 minute.
2. Drain the tomatoes and remove the skins.
3. Remove the seeds and chop roughly.
4. In a large bowl, add the ricotta and egg yolks and mix till smooth.
5. Add the tomatoes, parsley, nutmeg, salt, and pepper and mix well.
6. Make about 2-inch long and 1-inch thick croquettes from the mixture.
7. Coat the croquettes with the flour, then dip in the egg and finally, coat with the bread crumbs.
8. In a large frying pan, heat the oil and fry the croquettes in batches for about 10 minutes.
9. Transfer the croquettes onto a paper towel lined plate to drain.
10. Serve hot.

SUNDAY MORNING Sausage Croquette

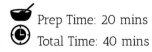

Prep Time: 20 mins
Total Time: 40 mins

Servings per Recipe: 6
Calories 530.7
Fat 30.4g
Cholesterol 309.1mg
Sodium 821.8mg
Carbohydrates 36.7g
Protein 26.5g

Ingredients

1 lb country beef sausage
oil
3 baked potatoes
1/4 C. freshly grated parmesan cheese
1 egg, lightly beaten
1/4 C. sour cream
1 1/4 C. panko breadcrumbs
salt
fresh ground black pepper
1 tbsp freshly chopped fresh parsley leaves
vegetable oil, for pan frying

EGGS
6 large eggs
salt
fresh ground black pepper
1 (5 oz.) bags Baby Spinach
prepared hollandaise sauce mix

Directions

1. In a heavy bottomed skillet, heat a little oil on medium heat and cook the sausage till browned, breaking up with the back of a wooden spoon.
2. With a slotted spoon, transfer the sausage into a bowl.
3. Remove the inside of the potatoes and transfer into a bowl with the Parmesan.
4. With a potato masher, mash the potatoes till smooth.
5. Add the 1 lightly beaten egg, sour cream, 1/4 C. of the panko bread crumbs, salt, pepper and sausage and mix well.
6. With 1/4 C. of the mixture make about 1/2-inch thick patties.
7. In a shallow dish, mix together 1 C. of the panko bread crumbs chopped parsley.
8. Coat the croquettes with the panko mixture evenly.
9. In a heavy bottomed skillet, heat the oil on medium-high heat and fry the croquettes for about 6 minutes per side.

10. Meanwhile in a nonstick skillet, heat the oil on medium heat and fry the eggs in batches till desired doneness.
11. Sprinkle with the salt and pepper.
12. In serving plates, divide the baby spinach and top with the warm pork croquette, fried egg and Hollandaise sauce.
13. Serve immediately.

FLORIDA CLAM
Croquettes

Prep Time: 1 hr 10 mins
Total Time: 1 hr 30 mins

Servings per Recipe: 1
Calories 27.3
Fat 0.7g
Cholesterol 21.3mg
Sodium 87.7mg
Carbohydrates 4.0g
Protein 1.2g

Ingredients

2 cans baby clams
1 C. hot mashed potatoes
1 egg, beaten
1 tbsp lemon juice
1/4 C. finely chopped green onion
1/4 tsp salt
1/4 tsp pepper
1 egg, lightly beaten
1/2 C. fine breadcrumbs
oil (for frying)

Directions

1. Drain and rinse the clams, then press to remove the excess water.
2. Now, chop the clams finely and transfer into a bowl.
3. Add the potato, beaten egg, lemon juice, and green onion, salt, pepper and enough breadcrumbs and mix till well combined.
4. Make small equal sized balls from the mixture.
5. Dip the balls in the egg and then coat with the breadcrumbs.
6. Refrigerate for at least 1 hour.
7. In a skillet, heat the oil and fry the croquettes in batches for about 5 minutes, flipping occasionally.
8. Transfer the croquettes onto a paper towel lined plate to drain.
9. Serve alongside your favorite sauce.

Arabian Chickpeas and Chives Croquettes

Prep Time: 10 mins
Total Time: 25 mins

Servings per Recipe: 4
Calories 265.9
Fat 15.3g
Cholesterol 0.0mg
Sodium 341.8mg
Carbohydrates 27.4g
Protein 6.1g

Ingredients

- 1 lb canned chick-peas, drained
- 3 garlic cloves, crushed
- 2 tsp ground coriander
- 2 tsp ground cumin
- 2 tbsp fresh chives, snipped
- salt and pepper
- 1/4 C. oil, for frying

Directions

1. In a food processor, add the chickpeas, garlic, coriander, cumin, chives, salt and pepper and pulse till well combined.
2. Make small sized croquettes from the mixture.
3. In a deep skillet, heat the oil and fry the croquettes in batches for about 2-3 minutes.
4. Transfer the croquettes onto a paper towel lined plate to drain.

VEGETARIAN DREAM
Croquettes

Prep Time: 20 mins
Total Time: 3 hrs 20 mins

Servings per Recipe: 6
Calories   336.1
Fat   2.2g
Cholesterol   0.0mg
Sodium   239.4mg
Carbohydrates   69.9g
Protein   11.8g

Ingredients

4 stalks celery, chopped
1 large carrot, finely chopped
3 C. whole barley
6 C. water, with
bouillon cubes or broth
1/2 tsp sea salt

fresh ground pepper
1 tsp dried basil
2 bay leaves
2 whole garlic cloves
breadcrumbs (use if needed)

Directions

1. Rinse the barley under the fresh water.
2. In a large pan, add the barley, celery, carrot, broth and herbs and bring to a boil.
3. Reduce the heat to low and simmer, covered till the barley is tender.
4. Remove from the heat and discard the bay leaves and whole garlic cloves.
5. In a food processor, add half of the barley mixture and pulse till pureed.
6. In a large bowl, add the pureed barley with the remaining barley mixture and mix well.
7. Keep aside to cool completely.
8. If required, add the breadcrumbs to make a sticky mixture.
9. Make small patties from the barley mixture.
10. Heat a non-stick skillet and cook the patties till golden brown from both sides.
11. Serve alongside your favorite sauce.

New England Cod Croquettes

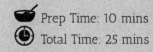

Prep Time: 10 mins
Total Time: 25 mins

Servings per Recipe: 4
Calories 486.0
Fat 18.8g
Cholesterol 113.7mg3
Sodium 547.0mg
Carbohydrates 44.6g
Protein 34.7g

Ingredients

1 dash salt
1 lemon
1 1/4 lbs fresh cod
1/4 C. vegetable oil, eyeball it
2 tsp seafood seasoning (Old Bay)
2 stalks celery & leaves, finely chopped
1 small yellow onion, peeled and finely chopped
2 - 3 tbsp chopped fresh thyme leaves
3 - 4 tbsp chopped fresh flat-leaf parsley
black pepper
1 egg
2 C. plain breadcrumbs

Directions

1. Grate the zest of a lemon and reserve it.
2. Cut the lemon in half.
3. Coat the fish with some lemon juice and salt.
4. In a large nonstick skillet, add about 1/2-inch water and bring to a simmer.
5. Add to the fish and cook, covered for about 8 minutes.
6. Drain well and transfer the fish into a bowl.
7. With a fork, flake the fish.
8. Add the reserved lemon zest, seafood seasoning, celery, onion, thyme, parsley, salt, pepper, egg and 1 C. of the bread crumbs and mix till well combined.
9. Make 8 equal sized patties from the mixture.
10. Coat the patties with the remaining bread crumbs evenly.
11. With the paper towels, wipe out the same pan.
12. In the pan, heat 1/4 C. vegetable oil on medium heat and cook the patties for about 4-5 minutes per side.

ENJOY THE RECIPES?

KEEP ON COOKING WITH 6 MORE FREE COOKBOOKS!

Visit our website and simply enter your email address to join the club and receive your 6 cookbooks.

http://booksumo.com/magnet

https://www.instagram.com/booksumopress/

https://www.facebook.com/booksumo/

Printed in Great Britain
by Amazon